Horrid Henry's week

GW00870486

Write sentences about a fictional character.

Make up five sentences about Horrid Henry. Describe a horrid thing that he did for each day of the week. The first one has been done for you.

On Monday Horrid Henry put a snail in the biscuit tin.

On Tuesday _____

_____

_____

On Wednesday _____

_____

_____

_____

_____

_____

_____

_____

Different characters

> **Describe a character.**

Look at the pictures, then write a description of each character. Remember to write in sentences. The first one has been started for you.

This knight is wearing shiny

armour. He is _____

_____

_____

_____

_____

_____

_____

_____

_____

_____

_____

_____

Homework Book 2

Karina Law

2

Lion in the supermarket!

> **Write a story with a familiar setting.**

Write a story to tell what happened when an escaped lion visited the supermarket.

I was just reaching for a packet of my favourite breakfast

cereal when _____

_____

_____

_____

_____

_____

_____

The day our teacher turned into a rabbit

Retell a story.

Imagine you're in Class Six.
Write about the amazing thing
that happened at school today.

Our teacher is called Miss Bennett. Everybody likes her.

Miss Bennett isn't like other teachers because she can wiggle

her ears and make things disappear. Miss Bennett can do

magic. Today she did the most surprising thing. _____

_____

_____

_____

_____

_____

_____

How to be a superhero

Write a list of instructions.

Write a list of instructions on how to be a superhero.

1 Wear a superhero's cape.

2 Always help grannies across the road.

3 Always _____

_____

4 Never _____

_____

5 _____

_____

6 _____

_____

A colouring race

Follow instructions.

Follow the instructions to play the game with a partner.
You'll need: • a die • some colouring pencils or pens.

1 Choose a bird and take turns to throw the die.

2 The numbers tell you how to colour your bird.
Colour the:

body red head yellow beak orange

wing blue tail green foot brown

3 The winner is the first person to finish colouring their bird.

Bedtime!

Put events in the right order.

Which of the following tasks do you do at bedtime?

 Clean my teeth.

Have a bath.

Have a bedtime drink.

Get undressed.

Say goodnight.

Put on my pyjamas.

Listen to a story.

Close my curtains.

Read the list of tasks. Then write them in the correct order.

Instructions for bedtime

1 _____

◯ _____

◯ _____

◯ _____

◯ _____

◯ _____

◯ _____

◯ _____

Instructions for cleaning out a hamster cage

Write instructions in the right order.

Write instructions for cleaning out a hamster cage.

1 _____

_____

2 _____

_____

3 _____

_____

4 _____

_____

5 _____

_____

6 _____

_____

New shoes

Write about a personal experience.

Write about your own experience of buying a new pair of shoes. Answer these questions about what happened.

❶ Who took you shopping? _____

❷ Did you have your feet measured?   Yes ☐   No ☐

❸ How many pairs of shoes did you try on? _____

❹ Did you wear your new shoes home?   Yes ☐   No ☐

❺ What did you think of them? _____

_____

Draw a picture of your new shoes. Write a few words to describe them.

_____

_____

_____

_____

Guess who?

Identify characters from traditional stories.

Look at the pictures and read the clues.
Draw a line from each clue to the character it goes with.

I like to visit my grandmother who lives in a cottage in the forest. I don't like wolves.

I cook and clean all day for my two sisters and stepmother.

I planted a handful of beans and one grew into an enormous beanstalk.

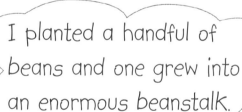

Now write a clue for the character that is left over.

_____

_____

_____

Royal wedding invitation

Write an invitation.

Help the Frog Prince and the Princess with their wedding invitations.

1 Write the names of the bride and groom.

2 Write the address of the place where the wedding will be.

3 Write the date and time of the wedding.

4 Decorate the invitation.

_____ and _____
invite you to join them on their wedding day

at _____

on _____ at ____ o'clock

and afterwards for a celebration feast.

Imagine you've been invited to the wedding.
Make a card to reply.

The frog princess

Use a storyboard to tell a story.

Write sentences next to each picture to tell the story.

Behind the headlines

Identify traditional stories.

Read each headline and then write down the name of the fairytale.

> **SEVEN QUESTIONED OVER MYSTERIOUS POISONING OF BEAUTIFUL GIRL**

> **INTRUDER STEALS BREAKFAST AND BREAKS FURNITURE**

> PRINCE SEEKS MYSTERY WOMAN WHO FLED PALACE BALL, LEAVING GLASS SLIPPER BEHIND

Write a headline for this story.

The life cycle of a tree

Write captions for a cycle diagram.

These pictures show a tree at different times of the year.

1 Write the name of each season and a sentence to say what happens to the tree.

2 Add the missing arrows.

Spring

The blossom comes out on the tree.

Making notes

Label a picture and make notes.

1 Read the passage carefully. Then use the information to make a labelled picture of a butterfly.

Butterflies are insects. They have four wings and six legs. They have two feelers on their heads.

Butterflies also have long, curly tongues. A butterfly uses its tongue to drink food from flowers.

There are many different types of butterfly. They have many different colours. Many butterflies have beautiful patterns on their wings. Sometimes these patterns look like eyes. They frighten away animals that might want to eat the butterfly.

2 Write down two facts about butterflies' wings.

_____

_____

Using connectives

Use connectives to finish sentences.

Read the first part of each sentence.
The words in bold are **connectives**.
Connectives link different bits of information.
Think of a way to finish each sentence.

1 Snakes cannot see very well and they
have no ears **but** _____

_____

2 From time to time, a snake needs to shed its
skin **because** _____

_____

3 A mother hen keeps her eggs safe and
warm **by** _____

_____

4 A chick has a special tooth called an egg
tooth **that** _____

_____

Delicious words

Choose words to describe food.

Write down some words under each picture that describe it.

warm   _____   _____

slippery   _____   _____

soft   _____   _____

squishy   _____   _____

tasty   _____   _____

Draw your favourite food here.
Write down some words that
describe it.

_____

_____

_____

_____

Comparing stories

Compare two stories by the same author.

Choose two stories you've read by one of your favourite authors. Fill in the chart and then answer the questions below.

Title	Characters	Setting

❶ Think about what is the **same** in the two stories.

❷ Think what is **different** about them.

❸ Which story do you prefer? _____

❹ Why? _____

_____

Sorry Miss!

Write a letter of apology.

Imagine you are Mildred. Write a letter of apology to Miss Hardbroom, explaining your actions and promising to stick to the rules in future.

Dear Miss Hardbroom,

    I am very sorry about my behaviour today. I was having trouble getting my kitten to stay on my broomstick. He doesn't balance very well and he kept falling off. So I thought _____

_____

_____

_____

_____

_____

_____

Yours apologetically,

Mildred

Author profile

Find out about a favourite author.

Choose an author whose stories you enjoy.
Read information about them on their
book covers or on a website.

Name of author: _____

Books they have written:

- _____

- _____

- _____

Which of their books have you enjoyed most?

_____

_____

Why? _____

_____

_____

_____

Wet weather words

Match words to their definitions.

Read the definitions below.
In each space, match the word to its definition.
Choose from the words in the box.

Word	Definition
cloud	a white or grey mist that floats in the sky
_____	a large amount of water covering an area that's usually dry
_____	the amount of rain that falls from the sky
_____	a forest in a tropical area where there's a lot of rain
_____	an instrument to measure the amount of rain that falls
_____	an object sent into space to send information back to Earth

rainfall   flood   rain gauge   satellite   rainforest   cloud

K words

Find missing words in dictionary definitions.

Read the dictionary definitions on this page. The missing words all begin with **k**.

Write the missing headwords. The first one has been done for you. You can use a dictionary to help.

A _Kangaroo_ is a large Australian animal. It jumps on its strong back legs.

A _____ is a small shed for a dog to sleep in.

People boil water in a _____ .

A _____ is a piece of metal with a special shape. It opens a lock.

If you _____ something, you hit it hard with your foot.

A _____ is a young goat.

A _____ person is caring and helpful.

Using a dictionary

Answer questions about an alphabetically ordered text.

Use the information to help you answer the questions.

1 What is a *weed?* _____

2 What is *wheat?* _____

3 Find a day beginning with *W.* _____

4 Describe a *whale.* _____

5 Which part of the dictionary do you think this page is from?

beginning ☐   middle ☐   end ☐

---

when

a
b
c
d
e
f
g
h
i
j
k
l
m
n
o
p
q
r
s
t
u
v
Ww
x
y
z

Wednesday   Wednesdays
Wednesday is the day of the week between Tuesday and Thursday.

weed   weeds
A **weed** is a wild plant that people do not want in their gardens.

week   weeks
A **week** is made up of seven days. There are 52 **weeks** in a year.

weekend   weekends
Saturday and Sunday are called the **weekend**.

weigh   weighs, weighing, weighed
Something that weighs a lot is hard to lift or carry.
An elephant weighs much more than a mouse.

weight
The **weight** of something is how much it weighs.

well   better, best; wells
1 If you do something **well**, you make a good job of it.
2 If you are **well**, you are healthy.
3 People get water out of a deep hole in the ground called a **well**.

wellington or welly   wellingtons or wellies
Wellingtons are rubber boots. They keep your feet and legs dry.

went   See **go**.

west
West is the direction you look when you see the sun set.

wet   wetter, wettest
1 Something that is **wet** has water or liquid on it.
2 If the weather is **wet**, it is raining.

whale   whales
Whales are the largest mammals. They live in the sea.

what
What is used to ask or talk about a thing.
What is that? I can't see what it is.

wheat
Wheat is a plant grown by farmers. Flour is made from its seeds.

wheel   wheels
Cars, lorries and bicycles move a ong on **wheels**.

wheelchair   wheelchairs
A **wheelchair** is a chair with wheels. It is used by someone who cannot walk.

when
When means the time at which something happens.
When are we going to the match?

from Collins First School Dictionary

Tongue-twisters

Play with language to create an effect.

Finish these tongue-twisters. Use words beginning with the same sounds.

Six snakes slithered slowly to _____

_____ in the silvery sea.

Barry Barter bought a _____

_____

Polly Parrot pecked a piece of _____

_____

The greedy goat gobbled _____

_____

Now make up a tongue-twister of your own.

_____

_____

Hidden words

Find words within words.

Each of these words has a smaller word inside it. Find the hidden words and circle them.

m o n (k e y)	pirate	computer	juice
when	giant	shelf	minute
chocolate	trumpet	witch	yellow

These words are made up of two smaller words.
They are called **compound** words.
Write out the two smaller words in each compound word.

toadstool ⟶ *toad*   *stool*

playground ⟶ _____   _____

supermarket ⟶ _____   _____

skateboard ⟶ _____   _____

homework ⟶ _____   _____

cupboard ⟶ _____   _____

Think of three more compound words. A dictionary may help.

_____   _____   _____

Spoken words

Record spoken words, using speech bubbles and speech punctuation.

Morris did not want to play. He wanted to sit and eat kitty biscuits.

Write what Morris is saying.

His mother said, " _____

_____ ."

A great big fierce lion wearing spectacles opened his mouth WIDE and showed his SHARP teeth.

Write what the lion is saying.

Mona said, " _____

_____ ."

Award for bravery

> **Write a certificate.**

Design a certificate of achievement for Mona.

This certificate is awarded to

_____

for:

_____

_____

_____

_____

Signed: _____ Date: _____

Book review

> **Write a book summary and give a personal opinion.**

Write a review of one of the stories you've read during this unit.

Title: _____

Author: _____

Type of story: funny ☐   adventure ☐   scary ☐

animal ☐   fantasy ☐   mystery ☐   fairytale ☐

The story is about _____

_____

The best bit was when _____

_____

My favourite character is _____

_____

I like this character because _____

_____

_____

Find out!

Locate specific information, using a variety of non-fiction texts.

Look in books and on the computer to find answers to these questions. Make a note of where you find each answer. The first one has been started for you.

Tips!

- Look up the animal name in contents pages and indexes.

- Look for headings and subheadings that sound helpful.

- Scan the information for key words such as "beak".

Question	Answer	Where I found the answer
How does a chameleon catch an insect?	It flicks out a long, sticky tongue to catch an insect.	*Munching, Crunching, Sniffing and Snooping* by Brian Moses
Why can a hamster stuff so much food into its mouth?		
Do snakes chew their food?		
What does a bird use its beak for?		

Food for thought

Record information.

Write down what you eat and drink in one day.

Breakfast

_____

_____

Lunch

_____

_____

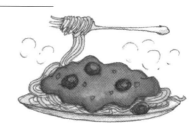

Evening meal

_____

_____

Snacks

Drinks

Published by Collins
An imprint of HarperCollins*Publishers*
77–85 Fulham Palace Road
Hammersmith
London
W6 8JB

©HarperCollins*Publishers* Limited 2008

Author: Karina Law
Series editor: Kay Hiatt

10 9 8 7 6 5 4 3 2 1

ISBN 978 0 00 722715 0

Karina Law asserts her moral right to be identified as the author of this work.

All rights reserved. No part of this publication may be reproduced, stored in a retrieval system, or transmitted in any form or by any means, electronic, mechanical, photocopying, recording or otherwise, without the prior written permission of the Publisher or a licence permitting restricted copying in the United Kingdom issued by the Copyright Licensing Agency Ltd, 90 Tottenham Court Road, London W1T 4LP.

British Library Cataloguing in Publication Data
A Catalogue record for this publication is available from the British Library.

Acknowledgements
The author and publishers wish to thank the following for permission to use copyright material:
Activity 1d: HarperCollins for the illustration from *Class Six and the Very Big Rabbit* by Martin Waddell, illustrations © Tony Ross, 2005 (Collins Big Cat); Activity 10a: HarperCollins for the illustration from *Morris Plays Hide and Seek* by Vivian French, illustrations © Guy Parker-Rees, 2005 (Collins Big Cat); HarperCollins for the illustration from *Mountain Mona* by Vivian French, illustrations © Chris Fisher, 2006 (Collins Big Cat); Activity 10b: HarperCollins for the illustration from *Mountain Mona* by Vivian French, illustrations © Chris Fisher, 2006 (Collins Big Cat)

Illustrations: Beccy Blake, Peter Bull Art Studio

Every effort has been made to trace copyright holders and to obtain their permission for the use of copyright material. The authors and publishers will gladly receive any information enabling them to rectify any error or omission in subsequent editions.

Browse the complete Collins catalogue at
www.collinseducation.com

Printed by Martins the Printers, Berwick upon Tweed

Browse the complete Collins catalogue at
www.collinseducation.com

Sustainable reading
www.harpercollins.co.uk/green

FSC + HarperCollins
Your choice makes a difference

ISBN 978-0-00-722715-0